THE BIG CHEMISTRY

BOOK ON SOLUTIONS

CHEMISTRY FOR 4TH GRADERS

CHILDREN'S CHEMISTRY BOOKS

Speedy Publishing LLC
40 E. Main St. #1156
Newark, DE 19711
www.speedypublishing.com

In chemistry, it is very important to know how something is going to react when mixed with something else. Whenever you mix items together you need to know how they will react since it can become an extremely dangerous situation. Read further to learn how to identify a solution.

WHAT IS CHEMISTRY?

Chemistry is the form of science studying the properties of matter and how it interacts with energy. It is considered to be a physical science and closely related to physics. It is sometimes referred to as the "central science" since it plays a major role with the other sciences including physics, Earth Science, and biology. Chemists are scientists that specialize in chemistry.

Chemistry concept

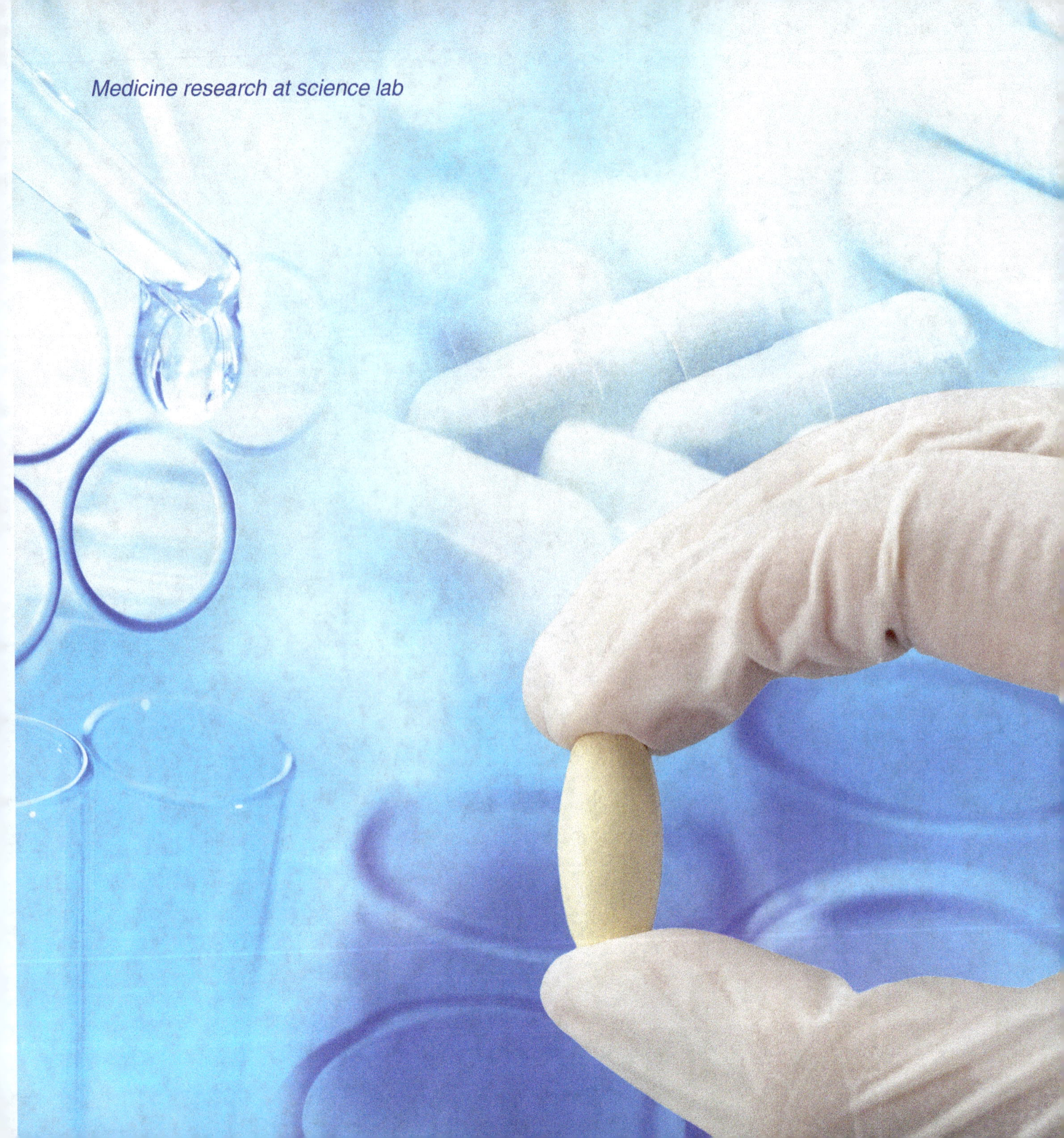
Medicine research at science lab

WHY IS IT IMPORTANT?

It is used all around. Doctors use it to create medicine which helps sick people. Engineers use it to create electronics including your television and your cell phone. Farmers use it to help grow their crops for our food. Chefs use it in making a great meal. Once you understand it, you can then have a better understanding of its many uses around the world.

WHAT IS THE DIFFERENCE BETWEEN A SOLUTION AND A MIXTURE?

In the world of chemistry, a solution is essentially a form of mixture that is uniform throughout. As an example, think about salt water. This is known as a "homogenous mixture." If a mixture is not uniform throughout, it is not a solution. Think about sand in water. This is referred to as a "heterogeneous mixture."

Sand on beach

Air is considered to be a form of
homogeneous solution

SOLUTIONS AND DISSOLVING

WHAT IS A SOLUTION?

It is a certain form of mixture when one substance becomes dissolved in another one. A solution will remain uniform through the process which means it is a homogeneous mixture.

- It is homogeneous, or uniform, throughout

- It is considered stable and will not settle or change

- Its solute particles are so tiny that they cannot become separated when filtering

- The solvent molecules and the solute cannot be determined by a naked eye

- It will not scatter a light beam.

Dissolution of gold in aqua regia

An example of a solution would be salt water consisting of a mixture of salt and water.

The salt is not visible and the water and salt will remain a solution when left alone.

Aqua regia is a solvent that can dissolve noble metals, such as platinum and gold.

They can be solid, a liquid, or a gas. Steel would be a good example of a solid solution.

Solids are typically more soluble at greater temperatures.

PARTS OF A SOLUTION

SOLUTE – This is the substance being dissolved by a second substance.

SOLVENT - This is the substance that dissolves the second substance.

Stack of sea salt on a salt farm

DISSOLVING

A solution occurs when a substance known as the solute "dissolves" into a second substance known as the solvent. Dissolving occurs once the solute breaks from a bigger crystal of molecules into smaller groups of molecules or individual molecules. This is caused by contact with the solvent.

In the earlier case of the salt water, the water molecules break the salt molecules from its larger crystal lattice. This is done by the pulling of ions away and surrounding the molecules of salt. Each molecule of salt still does exist. However, it is now just surrounded by the water molecules rather than being fixed to the crystal of salt.

Mounds of salt in Bolivia

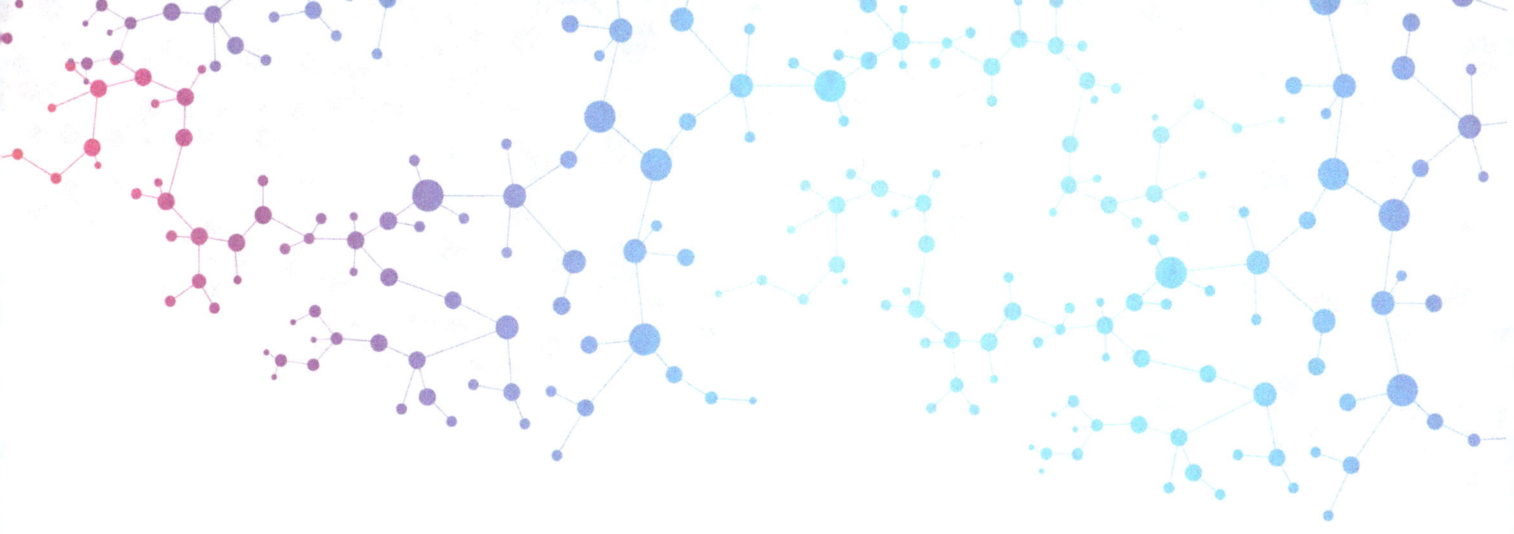

SOLUBILITY

This is a gauge of how much solute can be dissolved in a liter of the solvent. Refer to the example of salt and water. If you pour more and more salt into the water, the water is not able to dissolve the salt.

SATURATED

Once a solution reaches a point when it can no longer dissolve solute, it is known as "saturated". If the saturated solution then loses some of the solvent, solid crystals of the solute will begin to form. This is what occurs when water evaporates and the salt crystals start forming.

Salt crystals

Concentrated to diluted reagents

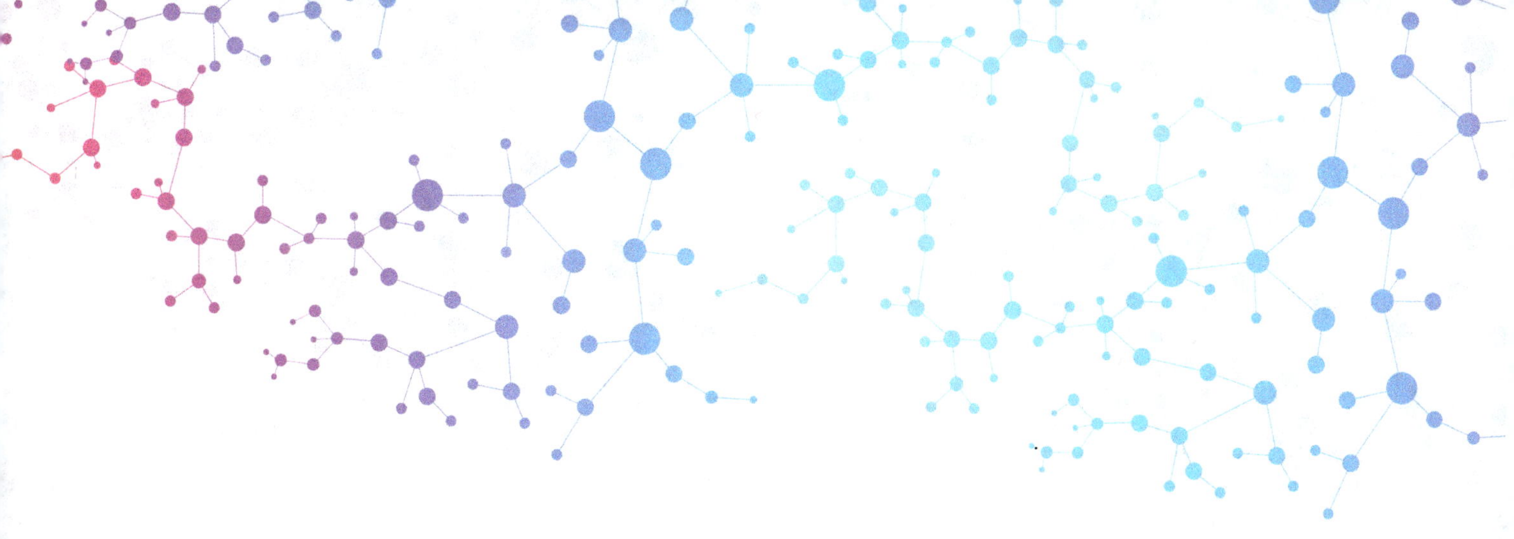

CONCENTRATION

This is the amount of solute compared to the amount of solvent. If contains a lot of solute, it is considered to be "concentrated". If it contains a small amount of solute, it is considered to be "diluted."

A can of soda on ice

CAN SOLUTIONS BE CHANGED?

Yes, they can. Many different things can change a substance's concentrations in a solution. Scientists refer to this as solubility. This is the ability of a solvent (water) to dissolve a solute (salt). Temperature also will have an effect on a solution. Typically, as the temperature of a solvent rises, it will then have the ability to dissolve a more solid material. Have you ever noticed that when you mix sugar with cold water it does not dissolve as quickly as it does with hot water?

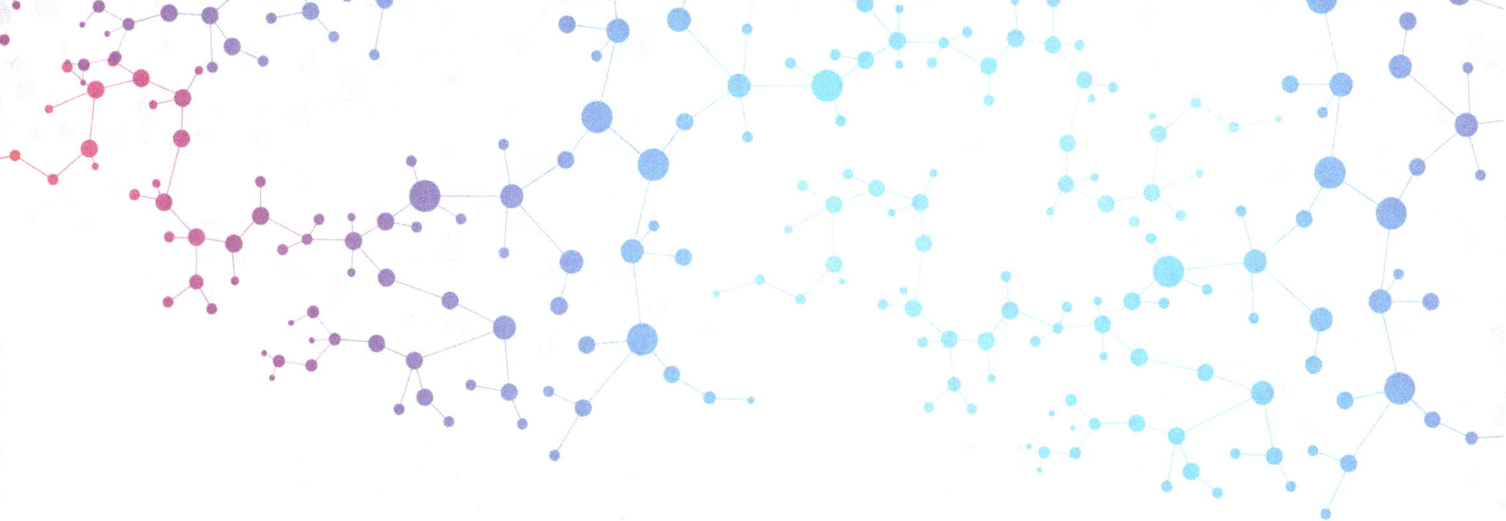

They can also be changed by pressure. As surrounding pressure is increased, generally more gases can be dissolved. An example would be a can of soda. It can keep its fizz inside since its contents are kept under a higher pressure. A different example would be a bottle of soda. When you open it for that first sip, a lot of bubbles come out. However, each time you open and close it, less and less bubble come out. As you opened it the first time, the high pressure was lost which kept the carbon dioxide gas in the solution.

MISCIBLE AND IMMISCIBLE

If two liquids are mixed and create a solution, they are known to be "miscible". When two liquids are not able to be mixed to create a solution, they are known to be "immiscible". Alcohol and water would be one instance of miscible liquids. Oil and water would be one instance of immiscible liquids. Have you heard someone say "oil and water don't mix"?

Oil poured in glass of water

White smoke on black background

MIXTURES

A mixture is the result when two or more substances combine, but not chemically.

General properties of a mixture include: its components can be separated easily, they each retain their original property, and the proportions of each component varies.

Smoke is a mixture of particles which are suspended in air. Tap water is a mix of water and other various particles.

TYPES OF MIXTURES

Mixtures fall into two main categories: homogeneous and heterogeneous. A homogenous mixture occurs when all substances are distributed evenly throughout the mixture (Blood, Air, Salt Water). A heterogeneous mixture occurs when the substances are not distributed evenly throughout the mixture (Rocks, Pizza, Chocolate Chip Cookies).

Chocolate chip

Aluminum rods in smelting plant

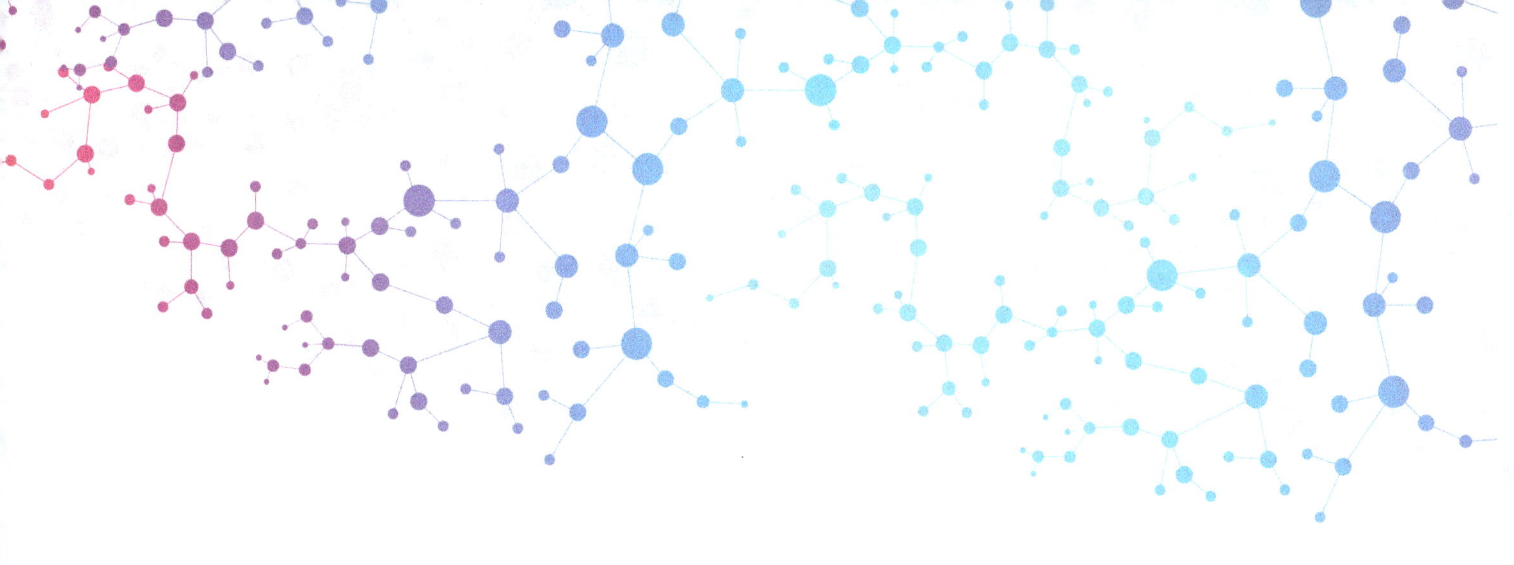

Within the heterogeneous and homogeneous categories, there are more specific types that includes solutions, alloys, suspension, and colloids.

SOLUTIONS – HOMOGENEOUS

A solution is comprised of a mixture when one substance dissolves into another. The dissolving substance is referred to as a solute. The non-dissolving substance is referred to as a solvent.

Solvents, oils, and spirits used for paint,
painting, and wood finishing

Cup of coffee - homogeneous mixture
is constant throughout

Salt collected from a salt field

Salt water is a perfect illustration of a solution. Its components have the ability to be separated easily by evaporation, retaining each of their properties in their original state. However, once the salt dissolves in the water and you are not able to see it, it is then distributed evenly into water. In this case, salt is the solute and water is the solvent.

ALLOYS – HOMOGENOUS

An alloy is comprised of an elements mixture having a metal characteristic and metal has to be one of the mixed elements. Steel comprised of carbon and iron is a perfect example of an alloy.

Raw steel on construction site

Particles suspended in water

SUSPENSIONS – HETEROGENEOUS

Suspensions consist of a mixture between particles of solid and a liquid, and its particles will not dissolve. They are mixed and the particles then disperse throughout the liquid. The particles are then "suspended" in the liquid. A suspension characteristic is when the particles settle they will separate. A mix of sand and water is a perfect example. The sand disperses through the water when mixed, but when left alone it will settle.

Styrofoam is a type of colloid in a solid form

COLLOIDS – HETEROGENEOUS

A colloid is the result when tiny particles of a substance evenly distribute through another substance. They may seem similar to a solution, but its particles remain suspended rather than dissolve in the solution. The difference is that these particles do not settle over time, they remain suspended or they float.

Milk is an example of a colloid. It is a mix of globules of liquid butterfat that have dispersed and remain suspended in the water. They are typically known to be heterogeneous, but may contain homogeneous qualities also.

lanthanum
57
La
138.91
cerium
58
Ce
140.12
osmium
[262]
prase
thorium
prot

Periodic Table
Bh
[264]
Hs
[277]
Mt
[268]
Ds
Rg
neodymium
60
Nd
144.24
promethium
61
Pm
[145]
samarium
62
Sm
150.36
europium
63
Eu
151.96
gadolinium
64
Gd
uranium
92
neptunium
93
plutonium
94
americium
95

THE PERIODIC TABLE OF ELEMENTS

The Periodic Table is how the elements are listed. The elements are listed by their atomic structure, which includes the number of protons and the number of electrons contained in their outer shell. They are listed left to right and top to bottom in order by their atomic number, the number of protons contained in each atom.

Periodic Table of the Elements

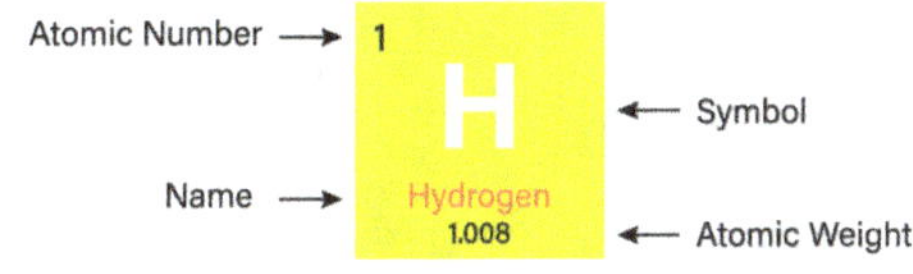

State of matter (color of name)

GAS LIQUID **SOLID** UNKNOWN

Subcategory in the metal–metalloid–nonmetal trend (color of background)

Alkaline metal · Alkaline earth metal · Metalloid · Noble gas

Lanthanide · Actinide · Polyatomic nonmetal · Unknown chemical properties

Transition metal · Post-transition metal · Diatomic nonmetal

1 IA	2 IIA	3 IIIB	4 IVB	5 VB	6 VIB	7 VIIB	8 VIIIB	9 VIIIB	10 VIIIB	11 IB	12 IIB	13 IIIA	14 IVA	15 VA	16 VIA	17 VIIA	18 VIIIA
1 H Hydrogen 1.008																	2 He Helium 4.002602
4 Li Lithium 6.94	4 Be Beryllium 9.0121831											5 B Boron 10.81	6 C Carbon 12.011	7 N Nitrogen 14.007	8 O Oxygen 15.999	9 F Fluorine 18.998403163	10 Ne Neon 20.1797
11 Na Sodium 22.98976928	12 Mg Magnesium 24.305											13 Al Aluminium 26.9815385	14 Si Silicon 28.085	15 P Phosphorus 30.973761998	16 S Sulfur 32.06	17 Cl Chlorine 35.45	18 Ar Argon 39.948
19 K Potassium 39.0983	20 Ca Calcium 40.078	21 Sc Scandium 44.955908	22 Ti Titanium 47.867	23 V Vanadium 50.9415	24 Cr Chromium 51.9961	25 Mn Manganese 54.938044	26 Fe Iron 55.845	27 Co Cobalt 58.933194	28 Ni Nickel 58.6934	29 Cu Copper 63.546	30 Zn Zinc 65.38	31 Ga Gallium 69.723	32 Ge Germanium 72.630	33 As Arsenic 74.921595	34 Se Selenium 78.971	35 Br Bromine 79.904	36 Kr Krypton 83.798
37 Rb Rubidium 85.4678	38 Sr Strontium 87.62	39 Y Yttrium 88.90584	40 Zr Zirconium 91.224	41 Nb Niobium 92.90637	42 Mo Molybdenum 95.95	43 Tc Technetium (98)	44 Ru Ruthenium 101.07	45 Rh Rhodium 102.90550	46 Pd Palladium 106.42	47 Ag Silver 107.8682	48 Cd Cadmium 112.414	49 In Indium 114.818	50 Sn Tin 118.710	51 Sb Antimony 121.760	52 Te Tellurium 127.60	53 I Iodine 126.90447	54 Xe Xenon 131.293
55 Cs Caesium 132.90545196	56 Ba Barium 137.327	57 - 71 Lanthanoids	72 Hf Hafnium 178.49	73 Ta Tantalum 180.94788	74 W Tungsten 183.84	75 Re Rhenium 186.207	76 Os Osmium 190.23	77 Ir Iridium 192.217	78 Pt Platinum 195.084	79 Au Gold 196.966569	80 Hg Mercury 200.592	81 Tl Thallium 204.38	82 Pb Lead 207.2	83 Bi Bismuth 208.98040	84 Po Polonium (209)	85 At Astatine (210)	86 Rn Radon (222)
87 Fr Francium (223)	88 Ra Radium (226)	89 - 103 Actinoids	104 Rf Rutherfordium (267)	105 Db Dubnium (268)	106 Sg Seaborgium (269)	107 Bh Bohrium (270)	108 Hs Hassium (269)	109 Mt Meitnerium (278)	110 Ds Darmstadtium (281)	111 Rg Roentgenium (282)	112 Cn Copernicium (285)	113 Nh Nihonium (286)	114 Fl Flerovium (289)	115 Mc Moscovium (289)	116 Lv Livermorium (293)	117 Ts Tennessine (294)	118 Og Oganesson (294)

57 La Lanthanum 138.90547	58 Ce Cerium 140.116	59 Pr Praseodymium 140.90766	60 Nd Neodymium 144.242	61 Pm Promethium (145)	62 Sm Samarium 150.36	63 Eu Europium 151.964	64 Gd Gadolinium 157.25	65 Tb Terbium 158.92535	66 Dy Dysprosium 162.500	67 Ho Holmium 164.93033	68 Er Erbium 167.259	69 Tm Thulium 168.93422	70 Yb Ytterbium 173.045	71 Lu Lutetium 174.9668
89 Ac Actinium (227)	90 Th Thorium 232.0377	91 Pa Protactinium 231.03588	92 U Uranium 238.02891	93 Np Neptunium (237)	94 Pu Plutonium (244)	95 Am Americium (243)	96 Cm Curium (247)	97 Bk Berkelium (247)	98 Cf Californium (251)	99 Es Einsteinium (252)	100 Fm Fermium (257)	101 Md Mendelevium (258)	102 No Nobelium (259)	103 Lr Lawrencium (266)

There is so much more to learn about solutions and chemistry.

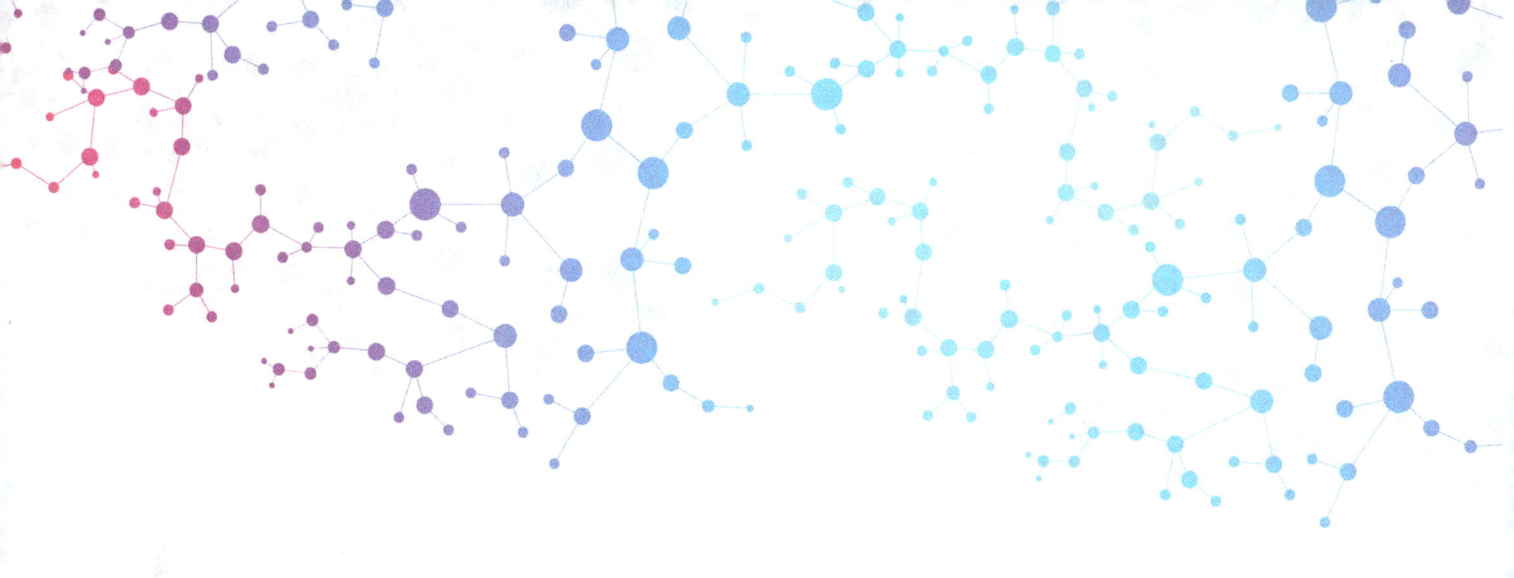

For additional information on Chemical Solutions, you can research the internet, go to your local library, and ask questions of your teachers, family, and friends.

Visit

BABY PROFESSOR
EDUCATION KIDS

www.BabyProfessorBooks.com
to download Free Baby Professor eBooks
and view our catalog of new and exciting
Children's Books